Quiet Time With The Lord

Jacque Waggoner

ISBN: 978-1-71600-590-9

Book cover photograph by Jacque Waggoner

Written for Christians whose greatest desire is for their life to be fully surrendered to God, to live in His Presence, and enjoy Him forever.

Dedication

This book is dedicated to...

My grandchildren: Erin, Hunter and Camryn Kelly,
Ben, Paige and Bradley Waggoner

Thankful

I am eternally thankful to our Lord and Savior, Jesus Christ, for God the Father and the Holy Spirit.

They have given me life here and forever.

They have given me the Bible, Spiritual Teachers and Friends in Christ.

I am forever grateful for my Spiritual Teachers; their lives of devotion and surrender; their faith, commitment, and courage. Because they shared their hearts, you and I can learn from them. We can be one with them in our Lord, Jesus.

Truth and Free Will

TRUTH

You were created by God and for God.

You belong to God.

Not to your parents.

Not to yourself.

Not to anyone or anything.

You belong to God.

God loves you with an everlasting love...

FREE WILL

God created you with a free will.

He has given you the freedom to choose.

The freedom to choose Him or yourself.

The freedom to choose His way or another way.

The choices you make do not change the TRUTH.

They change you.

Where Did These Thoughts Come From?

These thoughts came from the hearts of well-known Christians from years past:

A.W Tozer, Andrew Murray, Arthur Pink, Michael Molinos, Jeanne Guyon, Frances Fenelon, C.S. Lewis, Jerry Bridges, Dallas Willard, Charles Spurgeon, William Wilberforce, Oswald Chambers, Frank Laubach, Brother Lawrence, Hudson Taylor, Thomas Kempis, Henry Drummond, Thomas Watson, Jeremiah Burroughs, John Bunyon, and many more.

These men, like the Apostles, lived their lives in total surrender to Christ Jesus, their Savior, our Savior.

We can learn from them.

We can join them in full surrender to God, our Lord and King.

How to Use This Book

This book has 365 thoughts (one for each day of the year) for you to ponder with God. This book is a devotional and a journal.

Before turning to one of the thoughts, prepare your heart by praying the prayers on the next pages: The Lord's Prayer and Psalm 63.
Try not to just say them, but pray them, meditate on them, and talk with God about what they mean to Him.

Then turn to the page number for the day of the year, or search for a thought in the Table of Thoughts at the end of this book, or just open to any page as God leads you.

Ponder the thought with God. Ask Him what it means. What do the words mean? You may want to look some of the words up in the dictionary, or in the Bible. Ponder on the meaning of the words used in the thought. Ask God to enlighten your heart to what He may be telling you as you talk with Him and ponder together.

As examples, you will find a few of my thoughts throughout this book. They are just simple examples. You and God will have lots to talk about when you meet with Him. You will come up with thoughts together that aren't in this book. You may want to write them down on the blank pages at the end of this book.

Also, you may enjoy reading through the Table of Thoughts that are at the back of this book.

Enjoy your time with the Lord.

The Lord's Prayer

Our Father, who art in heaven,
hallowed be thy name;
thy kingdom come;
thy will be done;
on earth as it is in heaven.
Give us this day our daily bread.
And forgive us our trespasses,
as we forgive those who trespass against us.
And lead us not into temptation;
but deliver us from evil.
For thine is the kingdom,
the power and the glory,
for ever and ever.
Amen.

Psalm 63

You, God, are my God,
earnestly I seek You;
My soul thirsts for You,
My whole being longs for You,
in a dry and parched land
where there is no water.

I have seen You in the sanctuary
and beheld your power and your glory.

My Eyes are on You

Have you ever stopped, been captivated by the beauty of a sunset, a field of flowers, a wild animal? Have you been awe-struck by something grand, like the Grand Canyon? You, Lord, created them. They are a glimpse of Your Glory.

Lord, that's the way I want to see You. Show me Your beauty, that I may be stunned, fully captured by your Glory. Lord, help me to always have my eyes on you, to see you, to follow You, to bathe in Your Beauty.

Totally Yours

Lord, my greatest desire is to be totally Yours.
I don't even know what that means.
I don't know what that looks like.
Do I or am I even capable of understanding this.
How can I do something that I don't understand?
All things are possible with You, Lord.
It is possible for me to be totally yours, but only You Lord can make that happen.
Whatever it takes…
I am afraid to write that ~ whatever it takes ~
Lord, save me from my desire to understand.
Lord, is my desire, my will, to be totally yours enough?

You know me better then I know myself

You are My Only Light

You are the Center of My Heart

You Hold the Center of My Heart

You Occupy the Center of My Heart

Forefront of My Mind

Filled with You

You Have My Heart and My Soul

Following You

In Your Will

With You Alone

Trusting You Alone

Holding on to You

You Control All Things

Your Solution

Giving All to You

All is Yours

Your Love Poured Out Through Me

Shining Your Love

A Vessel for Your Love

Sending Your Love

Extending Your Hand

Loving You

You Loving Through Me

Pouring You Out in all I Do

Working for You

True Joy is in You Alone

Found Life in You Alone

Lost My Life to You and Now I Live

Here I Am

My Answer is Yes

No Details Needed - Who What When Where?
Not Needed. My Answer is Yes.

Offering Me

All of Me

I Will Go for You

You are in me. Where I go You go. There is no place where You are not there. Let me see with my heart and spirit those You want to touch through me. Lord, I will go.

Living for What Matters to You

What matters to You, Lord?
Your Glory matters.
Your Will matters.
Your Son matters.
Your Word matters.
Your Children matter.
I matter.

Praying for What Matters to You

Praying Bold Prayer in Your Will

Self-abandoned to You

Self-abandoned Trust in You

Self-abandoned Faith in You

Venturing Out for You

Your Power

Your Will Alone

Lord, give me an undivided will…
~ a will no longer divided between You and any creature
~ a will no longer divided between You and me

Lord, give me a will that never desires anything outside of Your will.

Lord, give me a will that never refuses anything of Your will.

Lord, give me a will that wants only what You want.

Lord, give me a will that wants Your wants.

Give me Your will, Lord.

Loving You with...

~ all my heart
~ all my mind
~ all my soul
~ all my strength

Trusting You with

~ all my heart
~ all my mind
~ all my soul
~ all my strength

Trusting You

You are the Life of My Soul

I Exist Because of You

I Am Clinging Only to You

Yielded to Your Guidance

United to You

Yielded to You

Owned by You

Silenced to Hear Your Soft Still Voice

Being Still and Listening for You

Rescued from Me for You

Saved by You My Perfect Savior

Calmed by You Perfect Peace

Helped by You My Perfect Helper

Led by You My Perfect Leader

Sustained by You My Sustainer

Guided by You My Guide

Healed by You My Healer

Knowing All things without Knowing Anything

Fully You

Silencing All Within to Listen to You

Lord, help me to be silent to all but You. Fill my mind with Your thoughts, with Your Wonder.

Being With You

Quieting My Soul

Abandoned to You Alone

Open to Truth

Learning Truth

Looking to See Your Face Shine on Me

Wanting You

Shine Your Face Upon Me

You are Lovely

Listening

Waiting

Still

You Are Everything

Accepting Because You Send

Being Purified

Gathered by You

Me Uprooted - You Rooted

Plant Your Will

Your Hands Hold Me

Lord, You are with me always. Sometimes I live like You aren't even there. I am sorry.
Lord, please give me grace to let Your presence be clearly known in my conscious and to be front and center in my mind and heart. Forgive me for being so rude to You. I know I don't deserve anything, but You gave me Your Amazing Grace! You gave me Your Son! You said You will never leave me nor forsake me.
Lord, Your flowers and birds are so beautiful! Thank you for sharing them with me. I love them. I love You.

You are My One Path

One Way

One and Only One

Following the Path You Marked Out for Me

Replace My Rebellious Heart with Your Heart

Worldly Support Stripped to Have Only You

Lord, we need worldly things. We need them to survive. You have provided them for our life and care. There is so much now, so much to "help" us. How can we know what is best for us, of all those things that claim to help us? What about medicine? It seems sometimes the "cure" is worse than the disease. Help us Lord.

Guided by Perfect Trust

Lord, You are Sovereign, All Wise, and Perfect in Your Love for us. Lord, that means we can trust You. Lord, You go before me and are with me and take care of all my needs. Help me not to be fooled by how things may appear. Help me to listen to You, my Perfect Guide.

Grace to be Guided by You

Guided by You Alone

Your Desires Be Mine

What do I desire?

Lord, I want your desires to be my desires. Help me, stop me, enlighten me, remind me, when I forget, when old habits and ways enter in that are not your desires, when I allow my desires to be the center of my life. That is your place, Lord. I want to desire only what You desire and nothing else. I desire You and You alone.

Led by You

Simple and Straight is Your Path

When the path is unclear, and confusion sets in, Lord, stop me in my tracks, for I am headed the wrong way. Lord, You say Your Way is Simple and Straight. What peace that brings to my heart. You have made Your Path clear. Help me, Lord. Help my family. Help Your people. Help us to stop when we begin to get confused and off Your Perfect Path.

~ Simple
~ Straight

~ Your Path

Emptied of Self

What is "self"?

Worldly stuff, influence, things that pass away...
Lord, sweep it away. Clean it out! All of it!

Ready to be Led by You

Stopped Wanting Answers - You Are The Answer

Done Arguing with Myself - Turned to You

Left My Desires to Have Yours

Desire You

Abandoned to You - Your Providence

Wisdom is Only Found in Your Presence

Adoring the Depths of Your Wisdom

Adoring You

Free from Me to be Free in You

You are My One Aim

My One Focus

My All

My Center

Silently Nourished in You

I Love You

Attaching My Soul to You Alone - Never to Your Gifts

Attached to You

You Alone

All of Me is Lost in You

When All of Me is Lost in You - All is Gained

All is Gained in You

One. Together. The Same.

My Soul is One with You

In You Waters Beneath the Storm are Calm

Refreshed by Your Presence

Only with You Joy and Peace are Found

Everything for You

All for You

My Heart is Turned toward You Always

You Enrich My Soul

You Fill My Heart with All Things Good

You Fill

One Aim

Only Aim is You

Single Aim - You

Pleasing You

My Single Desire is to be One with You

All Aimed at You

All Things in Your Hands

You are My Main Aim

I Only Desire what You Desire

Entirely Set Apart for You

You are the Peace of My Soul

Light of Your Path

Lord, don't light my path.
Show me how to walk in the Light of Your Path.

Your Way is Simple Lovely Quiet

Your Way

My Life is Simple Relaxed and Free in You

Relying on You for All

Only You for You Alone

Because I love You I want to please You

Eternally Grateful for You

Coming to You for You Alone

Coming to You - My Healer

Coming to You - My Wisdom

Coming to You - My Helper

Coming to You - My Answer

You are The Answer

Lord, when I am looking for an answer, I ask You to show me the way. I wait on You to give me the answer. I look for Your signs. Sometimes I am not sure if You want me to choose this or that. Sometime I get confused and do not know which answer is from You.

What I have not realized is that You are the Answer!
I already have the only Answer that matters, and that is You.

You are All I Need

You are The Answer to All things

You are My Answer

In You Alone

Relying Solely on You for All Things

You Fight for Me

Still and Knowing You

Lord, help me to be still in all of me, my mind, my senses, my all; so that I can hear You and know You.

Looking to You

Constant in You

My Joy

My Honor

My God

My Lord

My Salvation

The First & Last

I am Delivered & Restored

You are My Blessed Love

Uncreated Trinity

Full Rest is Found in You

Preoccupied in You

You Gave Yourself

You Gave Yourself for Me

I Give Myself for You

Surrendering All to You

Chose You

No Will but Your Will

Lord, Your Will is that my will is willing no matter what.

Rejoicing in You

You are My Only Treasure

You are Light in Darkness

Lord, whenever I begin to feel darkness come over me,
draw me to You.
You are Light!
Light is nowhere but where You are.
I turn to You, my Light.
You lift my spirit!
You lift me up to where it is light!

There is no Light without You

You are The Pearl of Great Price

Your Power is In Me

You are My Reward

You are My Healer

You are My Strength

You are My All

Walking in Your Path

When You were here Lord, what was Your Path?
~ getting away for solitude and silence
~ talking with the Father
~ talking about the Father
~ sharing the Good News
~ teaching
~ feeding the hungry
~ healing the sick
~ working as a carpenter

For You in Everything

Totally for You

Your Power in Me

For You

For You and Only You

For You Alone

Just You

Rested

Softened

Pure & Intense Desire Toward You

Only You

Lost - But Found

My Only Love

You Remember Me

You Have Time for Me

Saved

From the Depths of My Heart

Lord, What is Your Favorite Color?

You You You

Your Other Thoughts with God

Table of Thoughts

My Eyes are on You 1
Totally Yours 2
You know me better then I know myself 3
You are My Only Light 4
You are the Center of My Heart 5
You Hold the Center of My Heart 6
You Occupy the Center of My Heart 7
Forefront of My Mind 8
Filled with You 9
You Have My Heart and My Soul 10
Following You 11
In Your Will 12
With You Alone 13
Trusting You Alone 14
Holding on to You 15
You Control All Things 16
Your Solution 17
Clinging to You 18
Giving All to You 19
All is Yours 20
Your Love Poured Out Through Me 21
Shining Your Love 22
A Vessel for Your Love 23
Sending Your Love 24

Extending Your Hand........25
Loving You........26
You Loving Through Me........27
Clinging to The Anchor of My Soul........28
Radiating Your Light........29
Unleashing Your Power Through Me........30
Living for You Alone........31
Pouring You Out in all I Do........32
Working for You........33
True Joy is in You Alone........34
Found Life in You Alone........35
Thinking Big in You........36
Lost My Life to You and Now I Live........37
Send Me Lord........38
Here I Am........39
My Answer is Yes........40
Here I Am, Send Me........41
No Details Needed - Who What When Where? Not Needed. My Answer is Yes........42
Offering Me........43
All of Me........44
I Will Go for You........45
Living for What Matters to You........46
Praying for What Matters to You........47
Praying Your Will........48
Praying Bold Prayer in Your Will........49

Recklessly Pursuing You.. 50
Self-abandoned to You.. 51
Self-abandoned Trust in You.. 52
Self-abandoned Faith in You.. 53
Venturing Out for You.. 54
Dreaming Big in You.. 55
Daring & Believing in You.. 56
Your Power.. 57
Life Matters Only in You.. 58
Your Will Alone.. 59
Loving You with….. 60
Trusting You with.. 61
Loving for the Love of You.. 62
Every Step with You.. 63
Trusting You.. 64
Your Will ~ Not Mine.. 65
Depending on You Alone.. 66
You are the Life of My Soul.. 67
I Exist Because of You.. 68
I Am Clinging Only to You.. 69
Given a Heart Like Yours.. 70
Life of My Soul.. 71
Yielded to Your Guidance.. 72
United to You.. 73
Yielded to You.. 74
Surrendered to You.. 75

One with You.. 76
Lost in You.. 77
Guided by You.. 78
Owned by You... 79
Fully Relying on You... 80
Silenced to Hear Your Soft Still Voice............................... 81
You Have the Words of Eternal Life................................... 82
The Soul of My Soul.. 83
Love of My Soul.. 84
Being Still and Listening for You.................................... 85
Hearing You Alone.. 86
Simply Willing... 87
Open to You Alone.. 88
Simple ~ Your Secret... 89
Abandoned to Your Grace.. 90
Rescued from Me for You.. 91
Following You My Perfect Guide....................................... 92
Saved by You My Perfect Savior....................................... 93
Taught by You My Perfect Teacher..................................... 94
Calmed by You Perfect Peace.. 95
Helped by You My Perfect Helper...................................... 96
Led by You My Perfect Leader... 97
Known by You My Creator.. 98
Sustained by You My Sustainer.. 99
Am Because of You.. 100
Guided by You My Guide... 101

Healed by You My Healer 102
Knowing All things without Knowing Anything 103
Nothing but You 104
Fully You 105
Silencing All Within to Listen to You 106
Being With You 107
Talking With You 108
Quieting My Soul 109
Listening to You Alone 110
Abandoned to You Alone 111
Open to Truth 112
Learning Truth 113
Moment by Moment 114
Looking to See Your Face Shine on Me 115
Wanting You 116
Shine Your Face Upon Me 117
You are Precious to Me 118
You are My Treasure 119
You are Lovely 120
Listening 121
Waiting 122
Still 123
All Truth 124
You Are Everything 125
You Do Everything 126
Accepting Because You Send 127

Flexible to Your Design of Grace 128
Being Purified 129
Gathered by You 130
Me Uprooted - You Rooted 131
Uproot My Will 132
Plant Your Will 133
Your Hands Hold Me 134
Strong in You 135
You Became Weak, so I Could Be Saved 136
You Became Weak, so I Could Be Strong 137
Living with You in Everything 138
You are My One Path 139
One Way 140
One and Only One 141
The Only Way 142
The Only Path 143
Following the Path You Marked Out for Me 144
Following the Only Path that Leads to You 145
Changing My Rebellious Heart - Your Heart 146
Replace My Rebellious Heart with Your Heart 147
Worldly Support Stripped to Have Only You 148
Guided by Perfect Trust 149
Grace to be Guided by You 150
Guided by You Alone 151
Your Desires Be Mine 152
Led by You 153

Simple and Straight is Your Path 154
Emptied of Self 155
Ready to be Led by You 156
Lead Me Moment by Moment 157
My Soul is Turned Toward You 158
Stopped Wanting Answers - You Are The Answer 159
Done Arguing with Myself - Turned to You 160
Left My Desires to Have Yours 161
Desire You 162
Left My Wants to Have Yours 163
Perfectly Free in Your Will 164
Abandoned to You - Your Providence 165
Abandoned to You - Abundance is in You 166
Finding Wisdom in Your Presence 167
Wisdom is Only Found in Your Presence 168
Adoring the Depths of Your Wisdom 169
Adoring You 170
Free from Me to be Free in You 171
Resting in You I am Free 172
Perfectly Free in You 173
Living in Faith 174
Faith Lives Here 175
Abandoned into Your Hands 176
Seeking You Yourself 177
Believing in You Without Seeing You 178
Not Seeing You Yet I know You 179

My Single Desire is You 180
You are My One Aim 181
My One Focus 182
My All 183
My Center 184
Silently Nourished in You 185
Loving You Without Desiring to Feel Love 186
Love Without Feeling 187
Believe Without Seeing 188
Loving You No Matter What 189
Loving You Even If 190
Loving You Anyway 191
Loving You for You 192
I Love You 193
Love You More 194
Love You Most 195
Attaching My Soul to You Alone - Never to Your Gifts ... 196
Attached to You 197
You Alone 198
All of Me is Lost in You 199
When All of Me is Lost in You - All is Gained 200
All is Gained in You 201
One with Your Will 202
My Soul is One with You 203
In You Waters Beneath the Storm are Calm 204
Refreshed by Your Presence 205

Only with You Joy and Peace are Found 206
Everything for You.. 207
All for You 208
Keeping My Eyes Always on You...................................... 209
My Heart is Turned toward You Always........................... 210
You Enrich My Soul 211
You Fill My Heart with All Things Good 212
You Fill 213
One Aim.. 214
One Aim is You.. 215
Only Aim is You.. 216
Single Aim - You 217
One Desire... 218
Pleasing You 219
My Single Desire is to be One with You......................... 220
All Aimed at You 221
All in You.. 222
All Things in Your Hands... 223
You are My Main Aim 224
I Only Desire what You Desire... 225
Your Desires are My Desires.. 226
I Am Not Mine - I Am Yours 227
Entirely for You 228
Entirely Set Apart for You... 229
Not My Will - Your Will.. 230
You are the Peace of My Soul.. 231

Peace is Only Found in You 232
Freedom of My Soul is Only Found in You 233
Continuous Focus on Your Will - Not Mine 234
Your Will Lord - Moment by Moment 235
Light of Your Path 236
Your Way is Simple Lovely Quiet 237
Your Way 238
Walking in the Light of Your Path 239
My Life is Simple Relaxed and Free in You 240
Relying on You for All 241
Relying on You Alone 242
Only You for You Alone 243
One Desire - You 244
Seeking You for You Alone 245
Desiring You for You Alone 246
Because I love You I want to please You 247
Eternally Grateful for You 248
Coming to You for You Alone 249
Coming to You - My Healer 250
Coming to You - My Wisdom 251
Coming to You - My Helper 252
Coming to You - My Answer 253
You are The Answer 254
All I Need is You 255
You are All I Need 256
You are The Answer to All things 257

You Have all the Answers 258
You are My Answer 259
Persevering in You 260
In You Alone 261
For You Always 262
Relying Solely on You for All Things 263
Seeking You 264
You Fight for Me 265
Your Battle is Won 266
Still in You 267
Still and Knowing You 268
Entirely Yours 269
Looking to You 270
Constant in You 271
You are All Goodness 272
Boundless Wisdom 273
Endless Wisdom 274
Love & Sweetness 275
My Joy 276
My Honor 277
My Everlasting Happiness 278
My God 279
My Lord 280
My Salvation 281
The Alpha & Omega 282
The First & Last 283

The Everlasting..284
I am Delivered & Restored 285
Burning Toward You.. 286
You are My Blessed Love...287
Uncreated Trinity 288
Full Rest is Found in You 289
Full Restedness in You.. 290
Preoccupied in You 291
You Gave All..292
You Gave Yourself..293
You Gave Yourself for Me 294
I Give Myself for You..295
I Belong to You.. 296
Joy is All for You 297
You are Love.. 298
Surrendering All to You.. 299
Having All in You 300
Chose You... 301
Seeking Nothing but You 302
All is In and With You 303
No Will but Your Will...304
One Choice – You...305
Cherishing Truth.. 306
Cherishing You...307
Rejoicing in Truth 308
Rejoicing in You 309

Treasuring You 310
You are My Only Treasure 311
You are The Treasure 312
You are Light in Darkness 313
There is no Light without You 314
You are The Pearl of Great Price 315
Your Light Shines Through Me 316
Your Power is In Me 317
You are My Reward 318
You are My Healer 319
You are My All in All 320
My Soul Thirsts for You 321
Your Glory Alone 322
You are My Light 323
You are My Strength 324
You are My All 325
You are My Everything 326
Your Path - Not Mine 327
You Light - My Heart 328
You Light - My Soul 329
You Light - My Life 330
Walking in Your Path 331
For You in Everything 332
Totally for You 333
Living for Your Purpose 334
Living for You 335

Following Your Lighted Path 336
Your Glory - Not Mine 337
Your Strength - Not Mine 338
Your Power in Me 339
For You 340
For You and Only You 341
For You Alone 342
Just You 343
Entirely Enclosed in You 344
Rested 345
Softened 346
Anointed 347
Desire You Alone 348
Pure & Intense Desire Toward You 349
No Other Joy 350
Only You 351
Earnestly Seeking You 352
You Alone - No Other 353
No Other Way 354
Lost - But Found 355
Jesus, My True Love 356
My Only Love 357
Nothing - But You 358
With You Now and Forever 359
You Remember Me 360
You Have Time for Me 361

Saved.. 362
From the Depths of My Heart... 363
Lord, What is Your Favorite Color?................................ 364
You You You.. 365
Your Other Thoughts with God 367
Table of Thoughts.. 385

Made in United States
North Haven, CT
05 December 2023

45152468R00228